clinic

II

First published in 2011 by clinic & egg box

International (c) retained by individual authors and illustrators

ISBN 978-0-9559399-7-6

 clinic is grateful to IdeasTap for providing funding
through its Ideas Fund for this project.

Kayo Chingonyi's 'Red Shift' first appeared, as January 2009 Poem of the Month,
in *Tate Etc*. It was written in response to an installation, of the same name, by
Cildo Meireles and was commissioned by The Poetry Society.

Andrew Parkes' 'Juror #10' first appeared on *Mercy Online* as a commissioned
response to the film *Twelve Angry Men*.

Both Rachael Allen's 'An Expected Future Event' and Luke Kennard's 'The Death
Of Us All' first appeared in a clinic pamphlet as commissioned responses to
songs from Talons' debut album 'Hollow Realm'.

Book Design and Front Cover: Sean Roy Parker
Inside Cover: Hanna Andersson

clinic editorial and production:
Rachael Allen
Sam Buchan-Watts
Sean Roy Parker
Andrew Parkes

www.clinicpresents.com

clinic

II

clinic   egg box

ARTISTS

Stems.

Through the dark hallway of antlers,
dozens nailed high to the splitting oak,
she walks before strolling
out to the summer garden
with the nap of the lawn and, blowing
into jars says, 'candles, why candles?'

Although the flowers don't need it
she cuts shorter their stems and rearranges
them in their green glass vase.

Lilac and white blouses and pants
pulled earlier along the line.

He brings the whisky bottle wrapped
in the white serviette. They have never
jumped into a river holding hands.
Never have they jumped in a river and
only for peace does he agree the nightingale
at the fountain is romantic

Century Boulevard

Part One.
In which Jim Morrison describes a hotel where I once also stayed.

Atlanta has the most amazing hotel you've ever seen. You walk in from the outside and it looks like any other large hotel. You get in and you look up. It goes up about twenty-seven floors and the interior is like a Spanish courtyard. Architecturally it's hollow so all the rooms face each other across this vast garden arena. And the elevators are like, kinda like Victorian rocketships and they're glass and so you go up to the restaurant in the penthouse level and it's completely encased in glass and so you get this strange sensation rising up twenty-seven floors in this glass elevator. Oh somebody jumped one time.

Part Two.
In which I describe a hotel where Jim Morrison once also stayed.

Where's your hotel? She says.
At the end of the Century Boulevard I say.
Century Boulevard, bitch! She says
and we get in the car.
The boulevard is tree lined and true.
We get in the hotel and we look up.
We ride the glass lift up and down.
Albinoni's Adagio in G minor is playing in there
as I slide my hands in her jeans back pockets.
I see various colleagues leaving their rooms
on various mezzanine corridors which all face
each other across the vast space

the glass lift vertically hurtles through.
The beauty of the world, its desert sunsets,
their storms, are not visible. Its burning
farmhouses, its ferns' fossilized leaves,
its lightning, its cloud gapped ocean islands,
its goddamn rainbows half-circling barren trees,
jacarandas blooming on the banks
of the Merrimac river.
It's Sunday in the Bible Belt
And impossible to get a drink anywhere.

Prefers Dresses

She's popping grapes
into her delicious mouth
sitting on her foot
on the bar stool
with a fake pony-tail.

She steps off
and dances for funnies,
looks at me,
gets her giggle,
stops. Starts painting
grey onto grey again
and smiling shouts
'I've just had a breakthrough.'

Later I would see
her perfect tits
through a fish tank
sliding down shoulder straps
as she changed into her dress.

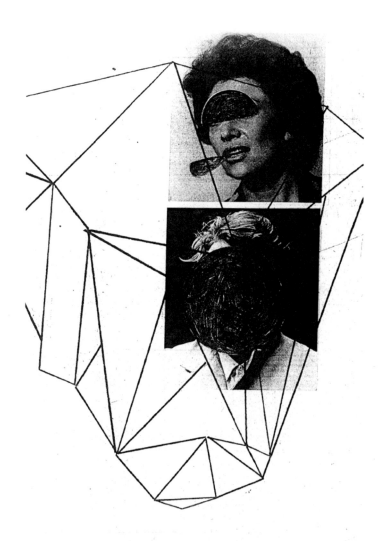

Malcolm's Landing

high-flown Malcolm   how to manage
precision of a landing   tail-ends of a time in pieces
flowcharts pointing downward

the plane falls in
its belly up   licked fire   appears
to unzip the sky in vapours   lost Malcolm

dimly listens with a telescope   to logic
predicting quietly
tries not to wake the day

he was homeward bound
when a red eye street stared deep
and it's a while now since we've spoken

he wakes again
the bones within his skin still sleeping
considers the last of anything interesting

Malcolm's Departure

the hour draws round   field-distant fire
oilsmoke slouching out
his fingerprints dust a corridor wall

watching ground freeze   he toes
a new patch in a snow
full footsteps are too loud it seems

an idiot wind is growing
his words draw further back   clear
like frost

disappearing in a frost
after music he found   his own footsteps
disappointing

Jazz Maggot

I

The lure, in that writhing red dress flicks back
and forth provocatively in front of
the sleek silvery breams, caught between sun
flutter and disco flicker, on the scales
of their fresh pressed tonic suits and combed fin.
They will grope at you maggot, leer with an
amber eye and bend slug coloured water
around you maggot. They come, flee, circle,
nuzzle you with thin brim of nose maggot,
tease and tow you in waltz, thin blue lips close
to your small face maggot. They are wanton
pushing each other aside, knocking you
in red heels to a stumble. You are ripe,
gaping, like a pomegranate, maggot.

II

But they don't know you wear a wire, maggot?
Recording each offence with subtle
tugs of distress an alarm calling to father.
as they rub the red garment from you,
sifting the dye from your skin with their scales,
nibbling behind your ears (if you had them)
silently tonguing the slug of water
that surrounds you maggot. It is too late,
the sharp restraint pulled as he takes you
into his arm jaw. You burst for him,
underneath that writhing red dress
he is crack-jawed in admiration,
he savours your final dance steps along
his thorny throat. He will die for you, maggot.

Mary, Mary

Not the sun exactly. More
A smear of marrow on the bone-
Grey shin-shaft
That has slid in place
Along the rim of the sea.
The gulls leave it pocked with beak marks, and are

Not quite gulls, but
Shoals of shrieking cuttlefish
Clicking against the cliffs.

Not wind as such – more
A general stirring in things. Net curtains
Drawn to thin columns
Strain gently against their hooks, pulling
On puckered tendons.

Up on the hill
The boneyard cannot keep its dead. They push
Their knuckles up through chalk. Shins creak like stalks.
Spines buckle, brittle globes detach
And rise like moons. They break the surface, loll,
A crop of grinning buoys on the hills' slow swell.

And up the hill my lovely
Comes each Saturday without fail,
Plucks the twitching carpal blooms,
The wandered fingers and the cockled shells, the pale
Fluted stems. Returns full-handed

To string them up around her nesting-place
My pretty maid in her house of graveyard lace.

Isis

Two parts epoxy resin to one part setting agent,
And I've a relic, sured against loss. A piece of you.
These parings are bright moons, lassoed in orbit.
These lashes configure a new constellation,
Fixed in clear plastic. Here's a stream of silver threads.

You are scattered. A house dismantled brick by brick
Is still a house. It can be reassembled. I have patterns
Pressed and stored in cellophane wallets, pages and pages,
But none so perfect as the one I keep here with me,
My jigsaw, my careless egg. And I have you in dominoes

Which I keep here with me: a bag of brittle runes,
They click and clatter like skeletons in the attic,
Like plastic trinkets sprung from crackers
Or milk teeth in a jar. Which makes me wonder:
How far do they stretch, the frontiers of you?

They didn't give me back all of you, you see.
Just enough for one grey dune. Which made me think
Of her, trek-trekking the featureless sands,
Picking up the pieces, no grain unturned, more dedicated
Than all-the-king's-horses-and-all-the-king's-men.

But there's so much of you! The greedy world
Has drawn you down plugholes in coarse stalactites;
The razor, grater, hoover, all wanted a piece of you
– Don't they know I need them all? Every scrap?
But my collection grows each day, my amber army

And I'll keep searching, mixing, pouring, fixing,
One grain at a time, till I've a heap.
By then I'll have enough to build that house,
Brick by plastic brick. I'll leave the door ajar
For the missing piece. And keep you here with me.

The Holiday Snaps

You keep them. They're too depressing for words:
A path cobbled with bottle-tops; rain in June;
Lobster pots and crazy golf. Bathers, planted
Like flamingos in the surf, conversation having failed
Years ago. A dolphin. Clams cuddled in pink forearms;
Iced crustaceans creaking on their hinges;
Cod in newspaper; a box barnacled with shells. You,
Pretending to enjoy an oyster. You think it's seductive.

An amusement park at night. The Big Dipper
Peg-legging the skyline, stark as a gibbet. The lost
Filling the slot machines; an off-shift Elvis, dead-drunk.
Fibreglass animals trussed in tarp: a jeering kangaroo,
A green monkey, winking like a concierge. You,
Kissing me quick, to stopper a gap in conversation.
That awful colour, like you've been parboiled,
Your breasts luminous, ludicrous as beached jellyfish.

A castle. Several parks. One in particular
With yellow cats: shrunken heads grimacing
Under bench slats, their bag-of-ankles bodies.
A row waiting for us at the gates. Tight mouths
Over supper; you, blinking back hot, furious tears.
Mussels in a restaurant – too baldly pornographic
To be funny, gaping deadly. The other diners,
Like a field of ruminants. A flyblown salad.

How did this get in here? Two years and half a world
Out of place: a hotel room before dawn; the sea
Gilling the ceiling, the bed, your sleeping body.
Vertebrae rising like polyps up the reef of your back,
Your skin fluorescing like a squid. Small discoveries:
The soft space behind an ear, the dimple in an ankle,
Miraculous as rain, before you forget to see them.
No, wait
                    – let me keep this one.

Khyber Pass Copy

Ice in glissando
up the pyracantha,
across the impossible
gradient of each thorn.

Let's call this the school run.
Pull out the Dragons' Teeth.
Creep past the hill stations
with their cottage industries:

Lee-Enfield, Martini-Enfield,
Martini-Henry, all home-made.
The gun mules trading on
 equal terms with the Viceroy.

This way went Cyrus and Alexander,
Temüjin, Timur and Brother Carnehan
bearing the crowned corpse-head of Brother Dravot.

I forgive Sussex for Kipling. I forgive Kipling.
I too am cutting my way through the midwinter Downs:

Red pomes
throng the firespikes,
sing, in their diminution,
"or else what?"

Gazetteer

'...with smooth-faced stone still holding back the trees,
nearish to a source of channeled water,
such water slowly working the stone pellucid.'

All that. And where the potshards
were few and broke at a King's order;
where Mycenaean, Hittite, Seleucid
provided for their envoys to be heard

in quiet palaces, where at most a light breeze
might be indelicate as to their proclamations
sounded with all the innocence of power
as children mimic bird cries in the ruins.

Sometimes, I'm Overcome Thinking 'bout

Everything is a bald or covert threat.
I am still baffled by Van Morrison's boast
of gunning down an old man
with a transistor radio:
Sha la la la la la la la la la la, re-load.

Red Shift

After Cildo Meireles

Take this lamp in pillar box,
for instance, first seen brazen
in a furniture shop's attempt
at a window display, a chink
in the glitz of crystal encrusted
bureaus, art deco light fixtures,
faux Parisian ambience. The flat
needed things, I was told, lacked
character. So, you see, I had to
have it. The fire engine telephone
came free. The two of them alone
looked off, somehow. I saved;
bought a persimmon throw for
the sofa which, alas, was neutral.
The throw too needed balancing

and who buys just one cushion?
It followed like this till my thirtieth.
Luca, from the second floor, gifted
me a terra cotta fruit bowl wrapped
in puce tissue paper. It escalated then.
Friends brought crimson trinkets back
from far-flung trips, even mother took
to sending sangria stained postcards
from her sojourns to the Costa Brava.
She'd return, with tales of broad backed
bailaors, to my front room and its new
acquisitions. Toasting my thirty-fifth
year, I held up a glass of *Diablo en la
Sangre* and, looking through, saw
whitewashed walls, the work left to do.

Orientation

Buy yourself a copy of *Labyrinths* by Jorge Luis Borges. Turn to page 83. Read the fourteenth sentence aloud. Speaking these words will cause a set of coordinates to be burned into the skin of your left forearm. Follow them till you reach a war monument where you will see a man dressed in a home-made lobster costume. Ask him if he has any suppositories. Let him guide you to a quiet spot where he'll produce an apple strudel which you should eat. Outside a '67 Pontiac Firebird will wait. Take the driver's seat by force. Under the seat you'll a find sheaf of papers. On these papers will be written, in a script only you can decipher, your original name.

Offering[s]

Our penance is measured
in mornings made to wait;

furrowed brows bathed in
relief bleeding from pores.

In this dance of coloured light
and pitch, lit wicks, set back

in sweat-flecked faces, flicker
with pleasure and pain, near-buckled

knees carry us to the crest of each
sonic wave *this tune is sick* someone

and everyone says, breath held before
the bass drops like a cliff-top melancholic

resigned to rocks. We deify beats now;
bent in penitence, arms outstretched

in this holy of holies, where all is a rush
to find space to make our offering[s].

Mostly deliberate ars poetica as a season

I write because my father writes
and because the other father
loved me for nothing. Too blunt?
Not blunt enough? Back in England,
oaks yell through amniotic snow.
The thinnest millions of branches
are born, are shaded white, in winter
parents discuss their summer plans,
because it is dreary now.
The poem's stink swirls about.
Cells mistake it for one of their own
and I grow breasts for a season.
Otters have flooded the chocolate factory
again and my baby sucks
on my sore nipple harder than ever.
It's the sugar in the air, I tell Frank.
He says the baby hates winter
just like his old man.
Why can't I dig out my thanks
this morning? It exists. I have felt it
before. I want to give it to you
for you to compare with, the way a son
brings out the face inside his father's,
whether or not they share blood.

This the real place

Below the mossy chapel on the headland on an indiscreet
ledge rock grass rabbit droppings sheer edge to the sea

we did it to embarrass the satellites since there is no God
to embarrass though not that in mind when we said

neither of us saying what for we would if the sun came out
go there: all purposes secondary to no purpose at all. It

in itself, singing to ourselves: private and lucky
to have the thing without the baby it would bring.

Afterwards I zoomed right in on the map and found
the nagging of nothing there but the long green bland

fall of the headland: it had happened where we
had been but not in this the real place on the screen.

Yes, She Seemed Demure

with her shiny harp-string hair,
the way her throat buttoned-up to mute. But I had seen
her eyes flow over like a vase beneath a left-on tap
and how around her, the men's patter stumbled
like a high-heeled walk across cobbles. No ordinary
girl. I so keenly wanted to know her, but she was unwearable
to me, with my overt everythings. One night I went home
to unfloozy myself, combed through my dresses
for shimmy and cling. Out went the showy. I shied my tongue
away from unbecoming talk, e.g. 'shrug' and 'toothy'; studied
my face into blank. Taking up smoking, I swiftly acquired aloneness
and never took a lover. I remember once she winked
as I glowered in a corner. We saw her less and less that year.

Wardrobe Ambitions And A Skirt For Peeling Potatoes In

Here's a dress for bee-stung thighs, a milkmaid's
flounce, one for fumbling in. Cuckoo! or the pop
of mustard seeds in a pan. Sass, like a splurge
of liquid pearl, like something about to happen.
Oh, my multiple futures – Peter Pan collars
and a Can-Can. (All pasts evidenced by a glitch of silk.)
No ballads of woe – a singing girl with a violin!
Come, sleep in these folds, latent with cashmere.
                              Did I demonstrate my shawls?

Kneel. Pick as many as you can carry in the stern-coloured
skirt. Gather your muddy hem.

EDWARD MACKAY

The Letters to God Department

[In] the Letters to God department of the Israeli postal service...
each year more than 1,000 letters are received and once every
few months [they are] opened, folded and... squeezed into the
cracks of The Western Wall.

The Guardian, *December 2009*

After twelve years on sector 14B of
East Jerusalem – four bags, a bike, a morning
start at 5 a.m. – this could be worse. In fact,
we're Mal-ach of a sort. Angels. Messengers
at least. The undivine employees of the state,
Jehovah's bureaucrats, paunched overalls

worn tugged across the absent space
for wings. The only angels that this time,
this place, this afterthought of history,
this former holy land throws up. We're
Noah's ravens, hopeless causes – that old
bird could do this job. God knows they need

a way to get some message through, to get
their intercessions checked and stamped beyond
this roadblocked barricade of disbelief.
We wearied years ago of wrestling
strangers through the night and dislocating
hips. We're out of the businesses of scriptural

dictation, flaming chariots, annunciations,
endless cosmic escalation. We gather up these
letters. Don't reply, of course. Just do
our job. Open. Fold them up, almost
unread. Readied, like the hands that wrote them,
for indifference, desiccation. On the bus home;

queuing; in the bath, the phrases glimpsed each
day reel through my mind: *from the depths I called
to you, O Lord... Help me pass this time and
I'll be good... Just take this cup away
from me... Please bless this house... In the name of the
Most Merciful... Dear God, I've always wondered why...*

Against Simile

However much I wonder what you are,
        this little twinkling star is not
                like a diamond in the sky.

  This ash on the corner of White Horse Lane and Mile End Road is not burned -
nor like a fist of leaves, frozen halfway through a wave.
              It is not a type of thing that sounds like knee, see, free, m

The sun is not like a ball of fire.
      Not like a game.
       Not like balls – which is not much like courage.

Wherever courage lives, it is not in the testicles
        which are not like a test tube.
             Not like the underground.
                Not like the earth – which cannot wait,
                  or be fertile, nor be a planet.

The sound of a brush against paving slabs
           is not much like £5.93 per hour.
A book of poems is not like an advance,
        a poet's pay not like a military manoeuvre.

Soh-La-Te is never had with jam and bread whatever Julie Andrews says.

      Brown bread is not like death or dying,
        (though bread is apparently like money:
        just another thing we all agree is like another thing
        against all experience to the contrary)

It's hard to make a monkey, pony or old rope out of cool, hard, bread.

We're told that G could begin

> greten
>
> gargantuan
>
> gash
>
> God
>
> whiz
>
> or an Air on a String – if it's a note –

Perhaps it says,

We need more milk

> or

> *I have eaten the plums that were in the ice box*

Perhaps if you drop an augmented 4th
(which is not much like dropping a piano,
or your ts) you will find something not at all
like the squished start of

> danish pastry, drawing pins, denial
> (which is not like the Danube),

> like

a likeness
is not like liking

as sure as eggs
is eggs.

Laura

Tell her, as you scramble from the lorry,
as she tries to slam the door, that you may be a liar
but you need her – her – to rule
your body, that you didn't just roll
from a musty pit and oral
straight here. You're short on allure,
so stomp around the garden like Lear.
Clown for her, rail
against the idiot you were, the lore
of your mistakes, the Erroll
double you left in his lair,
feral, tight, chest like a rough-strung lyre.
With your last reserves, tell her this: *your areoli,*
soft, hairless, your wet moss. I really think, Laura,
that you can save me. This, all this: it's not real.

Airport Poem

*she visits a disjointed number of cities... each one
the occasion for an elliptical postcard home to
herself* – blurb for Leontia Flynn's *Drives* (2008)

I get dropped in and fall for
the light of cities I didn't know,
because the tourism's more than over
– and that was never the point –
and catch a connecting flight
which joins city, home, poet, me
like some plastic knot of bunting.

Yes, the 'Berlin Wall' might be the
'Peace Walls in Belfast' and perhaps
we queue for the Louvre from the length
of Ireland. But what we take away,
is not the information, but the *taking away*;
the poet's continual call back to itself
like a token boomerang labeled: send, re-send.

And I frame this in my own airport.
I write back to London, from the airport,
from London. But I get myself confused,
mixing the plane that makes the distance,
with the omissions in ellipses, and lose both
somewhere in the blue air, and rather,
find my own home-postcard, and think maybe
postcards were never about moving, but 'home'.

SAM BUCHAN-WATTS

Landing

Stiffened by this bulk of ship
I am more party to its landing
than the self-upending: clean –
prising the strict rule of steel.

Homecoming has come undone.
Thick horizon block becomes,
not emasculated, but halved,
cut like a picture of a boat.

I stand rigid, watch the bow rise,
the inverted erectness stood top-ended
where it should be touching sea.

The new space gives room to pry,
whispers something vague about consistency
and in this short-term allotment as ship's surgeon
I think I know this hunk of transience.

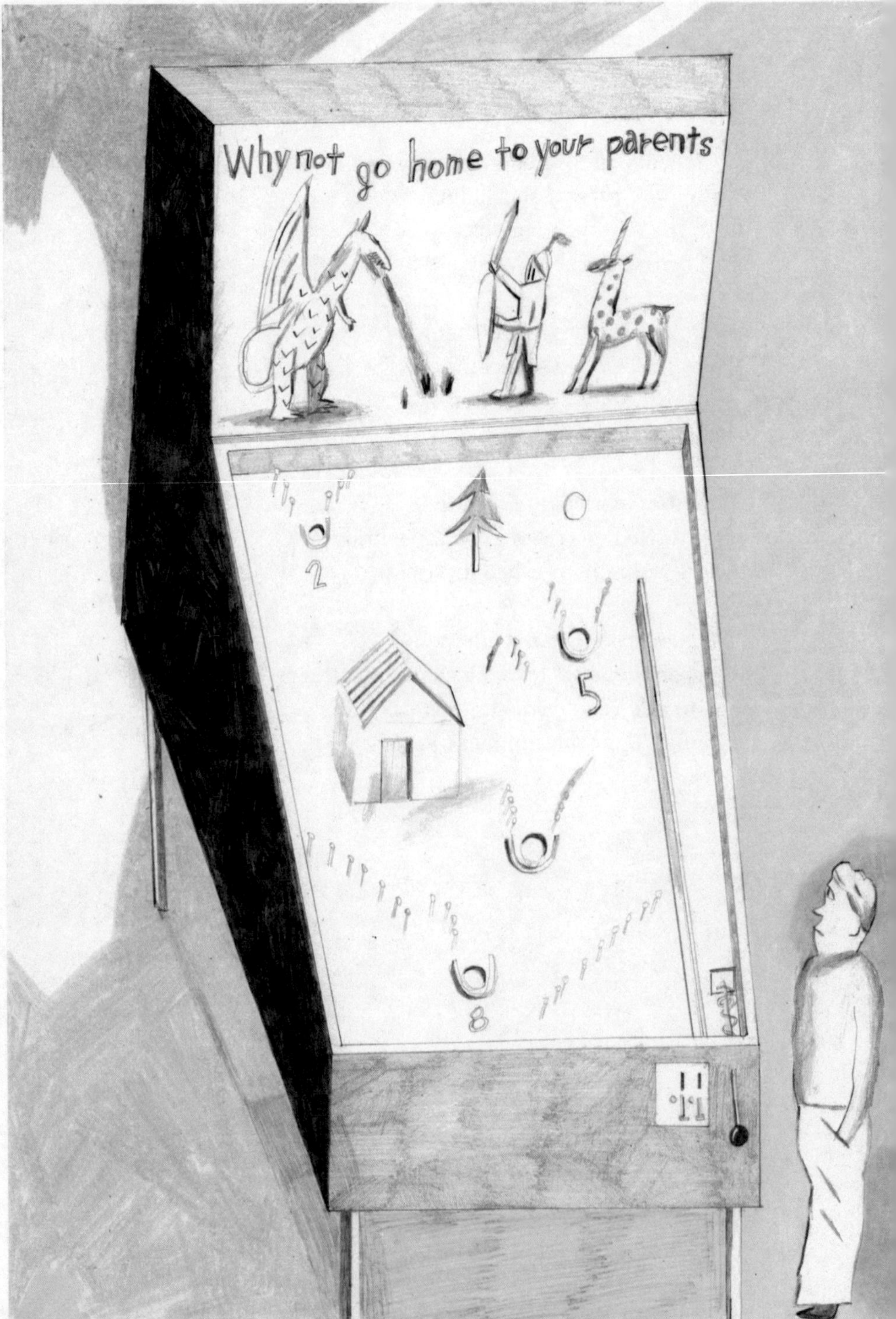
Why not go home to your parents
2
5
8

Under

I was picking an apple when it spoke
in worm tongue: *youth is busy in you* it said
and sure enough my skin greened, a seed-pip
lodged itself in each soft chamber of my pink heart.

Then while turning radishes, one pepper root
buzzed, a moth in my fist: *love will redden the veins,
and whiten the fluids* I felt it say. *Go home.
Wash your hands, for girls cannot be dug at.*

I walked the back-lanes where cow parsley dipped
and posed. One sprig I took and held to my nose,
giggled: *I am fed on the dead men of your house.
There is fog inside you.* I smelled my family name.

Lover, if I am foggish and truly dying, if love
fleshes itself wordily and I am young enough to say,
if blood has taken root and swelled me to a man,
take me home, wash my hands.

My other girlfriends

are all beautiful.
They say things like *that's wonderful*
darling, tell me something else
and my repertoire is endless.
Eating figs with one of them or another
on holiday, it's as if the sky settles in,
the ground leans to stretch me out
and the sweet breeze dizzy with bugs
conspires for me to lift their skirts
a little, so as to hold my interest.

And when we step out in various towns,
my other lovely girlfriends and I,
for an evening stroll before the dancing,
juke boxes singing from bars, a lager-top
fizzing, brightly earning condensation,
my other girlfriends multiply,
endlessly, beyond the grid of the city
into swarms of swarms of girlfriends,
so that nothing in the world is not love
or how it tips our lives up
and I want to see the freckles,
that are the enemy of dying,
on the shoulder of my girlfriend,
and only for her to be true.

I am being ripped!

Hot is the scene and autumnly the words
that mulch as I describe in the sun.
I am being ripped here.
I never should've come.

This was supposed to be my biggest day,
my speech before the Cardinal, the Judge,
the grinning Senior Prefect,
rehearsed to every beat and yet
they all sit ignoring me,
cahootingly admiring the Cardinal's new calculator.

I'm sure! scoffs the Cardinal.
Whatever... blows the Judge.
Is that all? slimes the Prefect.

When finally I'm done the sticky courtroom hums.
They sentence me to the square root of twenty five years
in a dog food tin
with a bad murderer,
and I will be downsized,
rehearsed to every beat,
ripped again.

Petra to the Swan-Pedalo

In 2006 a swan named Petra fell in love with a
swan-shaped pedalo at a zoo in Münster, Germany.

A sudden blow: neck glistering in rain-diamond
– 100,000 fireflies – your silver pedals crack
the water's surface. The glide of you ruined
me, made me game, webbed in this single lake

describing a perfect circle round your dazzle-
white haunches, plastering the cygnet-grey
air with ballads, crushing heather and basil
under my wing to scent flowering ice. Stay.

As our migrant kin ascend we'll sit and shiver,
forget magnetic fields, make Eden-on-water.
String me to your twine necklace,
                                        your sleek

breast; marry me among weeds, mid-river.
I will bear your giant sons and daughters,
my Pole Star the gold of your indifferent beak.

Natural History Museum, Beijing, 2008

Suicidal man being rescued, Beijing, 2008

Rush Hour, Beijing, 2008

Saleswoman, Beijing, 2008

Siberian Tiger's Preserve, Harbin, 2008

Collie, Beijing, 2008

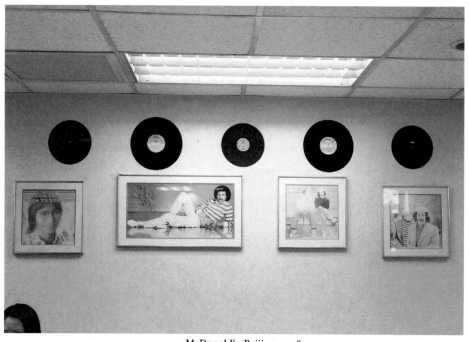

McDonald's, Beijing, 2008

Drunk Monks, Beijing, 2008

U.F.O., Wuhan, 2008

New Year's Eve, Beijing, 2008

'Modern Times'

In 2008, Beijing was chosen as the home of the 26th Olympic Games. and for Patrick, China became like a modern-day, Eastern, 'Wild West' where anything could happen. Protests ensued over the country's ties with Darfur and Tibet, censorship and the displacement of citizens caused outrage and all the while media coverage was non-stop. Many people are always on the edge of something, and the added pressure of the Olympics – the chaos, the anticipation and the oddness – amplified this feeling.

The story manages to enter the strangest, most intimate situations that sometimes seem able to sum up an entire nation's mood in one shot. China, a country that had fast become a super-power, was now on the cusp of another great feat. This was a nation about to tip. Or at least that was what people were told.

Mediation

Heavier than sodden wool, I know the wages
of petulance, how a hairpin can spawn
weaponry. I've lived this crusade as often
as a colonel stranded in foothills, making
sorry progress and executing one man
on each occasion of his private failure.
The holster was my great invention,
my mother tongue a dead language
spoken only in the crevices between
embarrassment and remorse.
So spare me the propitiations,
spare me, both of you, the logic
that would have us trust this as anything
but a cock-up of the first degree.

My Accent, the Eunuch

Old friend, I've watched you from the kitchen,
your mucky fingers running absently
over the moss, your wispy moustache
and undeveloped nether regions –
I want to hide you under my wing,
feed you rice pudding. I've given up
on nut-brown voices, brogues
for shepherding and frying fish.
I've stopped inviting them home.

Remember that time I tried
to sneak in one of my floozies –
a hooligan, or single mother –
and you wrestled them, with all
your dumb, deceptive weight,
to the floor? The love I felt
at that moment was enough.
I don't require tall tales, terrace songs,
the society of sots and punsters,

backstory. I don't need a neighbour
by the name of Phyllis, who visits weekly
to bang on about her shows
and an upcoming do at the Cons Club.
I'd be a liar if I said there weren't
times I prayed for you to teeter
and fall neck-down on the other side.
But look at you: your early jowls,
your vague feel of hippo, your eyes
as ugly as they're inoffensive.
You might as well come in.

Bog Bodies

Outside you all grow older,
Have a change of heart, move house in the summer.
But underneath, faces build on centuries of lost teeth
Canine, wisdom, raw molars, rotting
Jaws crisscrossing like jackdaws in woods.

Lost count of how long we've been here.
Can't tell a daybreak from a duskfall.
All I know is that I love you, enough
To deepfreeze, to rust, to plug my ears with dust

Wrapped up in bedcovers of earthy water,
We dream the mud of the bog, the dud of the wetlands
In our blood; stranded corpses scared in the pest house
Of young love, drowning in dirt, untouched, un-dug.

Somehow the animals don't find us; can't claw what's left
With fake nails and blindness. Can't even smell us.

We survive under the landscape. Dog-flesh, skeletons gone
But still there somehow underneath the peated eiderdown
Of the dead years when we don't speak.

Repeatedly pulling earth over our shoulders
We are neither water nor land, storm or stillness,
Like fishes that sleepwalk on mountains, horses that don't drown.

In a dampbed we wait between realms

61

II

Winter came like a cough caught in chests
The ground froze around us
Wheezy, breathless, still becoming bog, we half-lived,
Half-forgot. A rib-cage here and there.
A front tooth. Not a lot.

Not everything I touch is lasting.
Not even bogland
Not even men

He got up and walked away washing his clothes
Scooping the dirt from his eyes, unsheathing himself from
Bogteeth like a wet dog after rain

Only I remained. A set of eyelids sewn shut. Dreaming of mudsling,
The land being torn up

III

Spring. We are scalped heads. Lonely bodies,
Separately skulled.
I couldn't pull myself up behind him. Disturb the sewage of trees.
The flood of quietness around me.

So you all grow older without me,
Have a change of heart, move house in the summer
Leave me to imagine in the dark

Hip-bones, knee-caps, thighs
Outgrown body-parts

What's left is enough, you can rub it between finger and thumb,
It takes time to shrink wounds. To dry blood.
To knock seasons from the soles of your feet.

I let the bog hold me until I'm ready

Extract from Whalefall

There's this great weight I've been carrying round on my
Shoulders, there's shedding that must be done
An unpacking of my humpback, the misery
I've been storing up like fat.

Men dream of opening me up, men dream
Stretchmarks of the underworld like rings in oak,
The wormholes, the teethcasts, the crooked bones.
These are the bruises I'm left with – the birthmark love-marks,
Patches of darkspace clinging to more dark
Like trees scarred by lightening, lands torn apart.

Torn apart, I am mammal-showers, fleshy downpours, last storms
It'll take years to shrug yourself from my thunder,
Months of mothballs radiators sunbeds towels
What is this pain? This bloodrain, these hours of leaking.
Like an old house, gaffa taped, walls falling into the garden
A tear-duct, miles away, pulses through sand calling my name

So ripples grow and become something less dull,
Something throatlike. Water-voices, watered down
Shouts, mouthfuls of spectre, they stay eardrumming
Gravesong pulling towards rain

And more rain hours of it. Bloodpools. Breathless.
This is a soggy world. You won't get dry from it.
From this scrapheap drowning in your own skin.
You won't get dry from my saliva I lick bones of the world clean
Before I let the flood in, before I bring ocean to my wounds like
Hammering death-holes in boats and doing nothing

A blackhole tidal wave tent of skin freefalling finally cold-blooded
I think of all the water colours, the landlubbers and wait...

Simonsburn

When this comes

The yews like sentinels, divested of life, bristling with dull pods or cherries
of blood,

at the lych gate, in the city of the dead.

One day, I shall have a daughter I will call out *Hóney* to,   or *Oh, Hón,*

phonemes beyond approximation in the strict textures of print, half exaltant
or dramatic address, half strangulation.

Oh, the feminised rhetoric of pleading, knees cleft in the unlight
at Simonsburn, the poisonous frill of nettles purring in the wind.

Dire and beautiful is the male voice in its unmanning: Alessandro Moreschi,
Hostia et Precis, from faraway and through static.

Stripped of its sexual function, sómething cries through the open mouth *Óh,*

Óh, Óh, unrepeatably, consubstantial with desire. Believe me,
in the carnal paradise, you still can dance with terrific abandon.

When that comes

Carne

Body-raptor, beak embedded deeply in itself, yellow-rimmed caustic eye
fixed on its morning star,

the foreverness of night.

Please, imagine this as a Gyr latched on to its meat at altitude and falling

like a gyroscope about its own axis.

A Single Eye All Light No Darkness

Oh, Hón, Hón,

how sumptuously the dead resurrect themselves

at Cookham, yawning and stretching,

all time spinning backward:
in Boston I shall not sob

shrouded in clean linens, or else naked, genitals hidden
by sepulchres or yews, sun that is the first light of May

touching at the dew, the vestal rioting of lillies, goldening the whitewash.

Slow daytrippers on the Thames, Laurence Claxton at Gravesend:

in the grave there was no remembrance
of joy or sorrow after

if I can still say *in my heart of hearts,*

then in my heart of hearts, I am a Dipper.

Bank Holiday

Today, the is is at ease with what isn't.
The local trains not running, the wood of

the sleepers lie a trampled orchard in a line,
whose pale ghost-fruit now ripens on the track.

Unoccupied, we can choose what dream to open:
childhood, or expectations, or that often

raised lid of being somewhere else.
I sleep on my back in a foreign town

where the birds are blue and long-winged,
and folk are gifted in the arts of welcome,

greeting everything they touch and stretching out
to welcome first the midday, then the evening sky.

I'll stay all day here in this company,
then leave for home by the longest route

afforded to the daydream, and repossess
the days I make do with, the unstamped letters,

reminders of things I don't forget;
the ghost-fruit lying mouldered on the track.

Pigeon

At first, I thought it the most delicious noise.
Lodged in our loft it held forth its music,
one strain, over and over – as though there were nothing
in the world but song, babies, cake and nappies.

Friday, I'm half mad and cannot get out of bed.
The bird is nesting somewhere in our insulation,
perhaps she is so fat she cannot get out.
I wonder if she will ever leave.

By next week I will know nothing.
My heart will thrill like a tuning fork,
and I will issue forth one sound forever –
feeling love, love and love and love.

Cake fork
for Christian

An instrument unseen to him before now. It sent the soft shades
of the lowlight back yet softer. The idea was simple to grasp:

the cake, the fork, their proximate places at the table. And easy,
to clutch its delicate bodiless limb, lever it against the outside

edge of his index finger, to jig the light upon its joint with his
large thumb. He takes it to the cake, its scalpel finger investigates

the sponge. Already it is part of him – a branching – itself deltoid.
He bites, deliberately clamps his teeth, testing its qualities,

the temper of the metal. The echo of a pain calls. A glass bell rings
from a room at the top of a wide staircase. Already he fails to imagine

this instrument before he was shown to it, before it inclined to the roof of his mouth.

A Girl in Winter

My mother has reached the final chapter
of *A Girl in Winter.* I have watched her progress
all this August. It is like this starling's
across the lawn now: watchful, stopping.
She does not trust my book,

but reads from the corner of her eye,
as if slipping glances at a stranger's paper.
I know the last line: *Against this knowledge,*
the heart, the will, and all that made
for protest, could at last sleep.

Closing the book now, slowly
as a touch withdrawn from a feat of balance,
should a sudden movement upset it,
and the stranger snatch his paper back,
and the starling in the garden take flight.

Deco

I love you because you are like love
a flimsy and preposterous thing,
like a deco bedside cabinet
whose gold trim is coming away,
whose quilted sides are yellow and punctured,
but that you buy anyhow,
if only because, among the serious junk,
its cheerful stab at flair seems
a certain defiance, a retort.

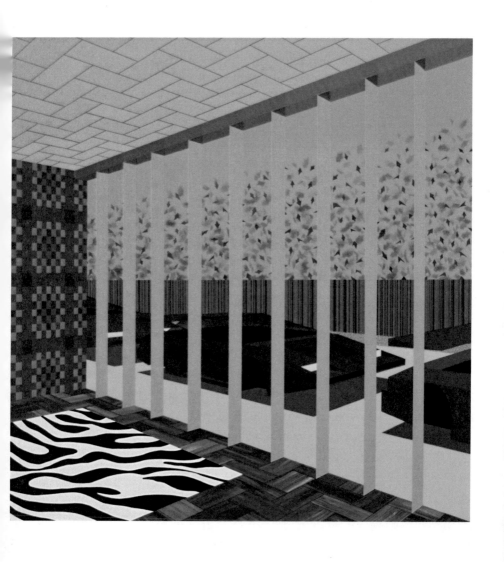

RACHAEL ALLEN

The Porpoise

We found a fraying half-porpoise
in a cave's mouth, stinking like a belch
with children grouped around in tribal circles
and sand-mites jumping in ceremony.

The sun set in fast-forward, layering over me.
The animal's other half posted solid on a rock
somewhere, eyes scanning like a lighthouse,
meant I threw away all my plastic sharks.

Stopped dividing by two. Took a firm grip,
when swimming, on my lower body.
Even when sleeping, I'd dream of stumbling,
and of its frigid head gaining on me.

I'd stare at the Girl Talk poster,
the one bordered by glitter,
of dolphins grimacing in Florida,
while miles away in the other direction,

in un-charted waters, porpoise heads
sit on black rocks, heralding
gormless futures.

An
expected
future event

is piles and the fact that
Carly Simon will always ring
from dark corners I will always
speculate on my first child's name
we will practise signatures privately
and watch each other sleep planes will
crash a woman called Marie will remain
childless no matter what she spends rap
music will remain misogynistic but we will
listen to it anyway you will breath you'll
stop breathing you will scratch your skin
you'll urinate and *whilst* will disappear
slowly from the English language (even
though a number of purists enjoy it) –
there will be purists!
You will fight
purist doctors over a cancer cure
for a son who will be sleeping

whilst a regret will grip you
as a sickness because you
can see all this arriving
like a fast black train
but you can do not
one thing to stop it
nothing at all
no nothing

The Death Of Us All

What had passed between us now looked like the colour-saturated
cover of a fantasy novel – and neither of us wanted to be seen
          reading it in public.
The embossed gold cage swinging low over the soft hills
as absolutely fragile as our belief in an artist –
a paper-thin glass snake in a cement labyrinth, the wiring
so complex it takes a team of five puppeteers to move it
as much as an inch. Three channels up and disrupted,
the disturbed boy sits with a 2,000 piece jigsaw puzzle
of the pyramids. He takes your hand and it feels awkward,
the way yesterday's detritus feels in your pockets.
The drama you wrote set between two wafers of an icecream,
the drama you wrote set in a Ford Fiesta's exhaust pipe
have nothing to add to this. The only thing you can help him
with is the jigsaw puzzle. Visiting hours trip the locks.
His parents are dressed as the dummies in charity store windows.
'Your father worked three years of nightshifts to buy that chandelier
and I'd like you to excise all sarcastic references to it from your
          oeuvre forthwith,' says the mother.
You can hear the wires snap, one every year.

Talking Panther

paces the room, his raised tail beating
in time with the grandfather clock.
His long claws click against
the polished wood floor. He wears a crisp blue suit

to compliment the iridescence in his fur.
His cravat was a gift,
from a benevolent tsar. His cufflinks are fangs
won in a duel with an Indian rattlesnake.

He tells me the panther is a solitary animal.
He tells me they are under threat
but they are skilled climbers.
He tells me of his scaling the Norwegian coastline;

he is the only quadruped to have conquered
the Seven Summits.
As he chews and licks at his words
I notice his gums are black. He never blinks.

He is about to recount an early memory
from his birthplace of Burma
when his perfect head bursts
into the greenest of flames.

After Snow

Left out, Summer's deckchairs
preserve their patch of green.
Two recline and one, half-raised,
regards you blankly, resting
on a splintered elbow. Looking at it,
you can still hear wild screams,
see the spray of water as it's kicked,
bared milk teeth.

The Mark

He knows the only way to fake emotion's
to fake (but not too well) lack of emotion

but not to get too tied up in its absence
(or, if you like, the pretence of its absence).

The last thing that he wants to do is hoodwink
himself into the thought he's hiding something

and leave his mark believing what he's hiding
is too conspicuous to be emotion

and too much of an absence to be something
he'd ever want mistaken for emotion.

Icicle

Always plunged, not swung as with the sickle
or ice-axe, and never ever ever by lackeys
but by oneself, pommel-deep into the silk
centre or through a window in the skull.

Notably, it is the best of all weapons to slake
a thirst for the mingling of cerain colours,
that is: *Burst Berry* and *Postcards from Alaska*.
Favoured by bust-hearted, headstrong killers.

Tongue

Never eaten, never touched, not seen behind
the supermarket counter with the rump and rib
or flopped onto the fridge shelf by a slippery hand

and shut away for what might or mightn't blab,
the taste of tongue is only what I dream of it –
a bulk of tentacle, all blubberous with blurb

which must be cut away to worry at the meat,
the meat, once liberated, full of fresh intent
and even after slicing prone to jactitate,

but prior to that, escaping the unvigilant,
caterpillar-crawling from your chopping block
then breaking into something like a bound-man sprint.

It must be gripped, and beaten for each urgent jerk
– with gloves if it's the kind with urticating hair,
which lodges little words in you that seem to tick

like timebombs in the sanctum of your inner ear.
Scalded, skinned and scissored into smaller tongues
that blindly loll around the pan and talk and swear,

the tongue is fried, its sizzling filled with half-heard songs,
names and lamentations and the odd blason,
the oil and juices crackling with faint signallings.

On tugging from your fork a sauced medallion
of tongue and your tongue meeting it, you'll find the sweet
blemish of tomato and a sour/tart tune,

a toughness as in toffee and the gentle blight
of turnip, then an afterglow of bitterness –
the taste of tongue being only what you dreamt of it,

the taste of tongue being only what you've heard of this.

Prelude To Growth

Tomorrow is watching today through the one-way mirror.
Something is taken from each, exchanged for something else, more
or less valuable.

Your too-thick glasses, the ones that
are totally off-trend, render the suddenly swarming pavilions
a tearful furnace.

No-one is more or less orange. Microbes of sand grow
on my eyes. The collision between cement-mixer and ice-cream van
provokes less identity

in the etiolated gallantry of longhand. Make milk my measure
of white. Or today a smaller fraction of my life.
To oil that lends water a gradient.

And yet the gorgeous weather continues to move along
the walls,
plucks the Dijon telephone, approves its endurance.

Now your hand hovers
over each object: it self-inflates to meet the bruit gift.
As these beaches

remain leaning into their own portrait,
in that fuller night, our skin powdery, we see the whole event
unfolding very slowly,

the wind somersaulting down our throats.

Apologia

His stillness knows exactly what it wants. Flemish, it climbs
down the rungs of its laughter, til strasse-light chokes
in the key of its throat, or a reticulated fog catches
in the youngish trees, or, through the milk-bottle glaucoma
of a villainous monocle, it scouts out the gallery of a plot-hatchery
with a test-tube full of unnamed molecules. Thwarted! In the long hiss of its head,
thawing silence slakes the fossilising song *Their Life is Hidden with God.*

Some song! Like a soft cymbal it shirrs in the recollection.
The city's plushness crab-hands along the neck
of its buildings. Who trusts such plushness, huh? (Does *who* fuck?)
It neither declares intentions nor inters declensions.
Playing it backwards reveals a song being force-fed itself (the *tack-tock-tuck-tick*
of drool from its mouth). Scuppered, he lounges against the scene-stripping
window: tries to name, then count, then watch, the flux of birds palpitating

in the sprained lens of a lake, a jigsaw shaken out of its box,
indicating, in a shaky hand, that the shape's clear, the picture less so.
Cheap tricks earn cheap treats, *brother,* he mutters, before, like the sudden urge to
feign sleep, an obscure and untrustworthy impulse selects
the sensation, then turns it over to itself: do what you have to, (Baltimore, *simpatico*)
but make it quick. But his stillness could outrun itself. Decades without water!
Then: We don't seem to have moved. *Then*: Every move an altar.

Juror #10

The head squatted on the thorax swells
a rancid octopus in monochrome heat:
deflated balloon under the churning fan.

Sweat creams in cabbage-skin
while Theseus's lifeline, the tie,
overflows his puckered tendril-throat
dividing the chest;

the argument tentacled in rippling
sucker-knuckles doubles back,
brine greying the shirt in smears –
collars loosened, armpits greasy.

Words bubble in flesh of foreskin-softness,
delineating the stasis:

I've known a couple who were OK,
but that's the exception, y'know?
I know all about them, listen to me,
they're no good.

The monstrous head –
arms flopping on the table,
upsetting the mugs – dribbles
bad language on shirtfronts
mazes turning back in ink.

The others then, trickle away,
interlocutors interlocked, walling
the flaccid cephalopod
crying at the maze's core,
arms mired in spirals,
fan-blades endlessly turning

Cockermouth

19/11/2009

The town tore like a retching throat –
abscessed bridges and aftertaste:
acrid flour, batteries.

Books drafted in the soak-up
doubled to Joycean proportions,
wet pages blending;

wool – swimming in the unravelling
river – knotted beneath the rush:
patchworked dark.

As the flood finally drained
snagged threads rose from the water,
swaying in the sun,
stitching the town back together.

Discovering the Early Humans

Under

We reached what they called Hades with long drills,
breaking the earth's igneous rocks into biscuit.
We were surprised by our lack of mishaps, how shallow
the first reaches of it were. No spitting wells
or spawn; or lakes of blood; nor chambers of white hate.
We lowered our wires, went down one hollow
into another that spanned into a blue panelled room.
At a dresser, the Overseer, reading, with his legs crossed.
You have come with the contract? No, I see
you are not the others, who are to assume my home.
He was an elderly ram, in pointy slippers, a formal tux—
withered, eyes turned in from each dim century.
We were disappointed by his wit, how plausible he was,
how young his face turned when we got up close.

Interior

On certain cans of sweet, sparkling liquid
there were smiling mascots just like themselves.
We tested these syrups, over a thousand years old,
and found them chemical. We dug them from mud
or nearly exploded from a food depot's shelves,
the ceiling's low backbones broken and caved.
Under there, one of our squadron, one of the best
among us, came sweating from the sodium aisles.
He held a little silver can. The can spelt, *Sprite*
and was open, popping, spluttering, possessed
by a voice that fizzed and spoke streams of bubbles.
It began to address us. It was a man's tiny spirit.
Leave now, it said, *before you finish up like me,*
repeating and repeating yourself, endlessly.

An Audience On Video

They say you can't see an audience from the stage
But looking back over the jellied images, washed and wrung out
Over years of play, the stars shone.
There they were – newsreaders, humorists, sportsmen,
And their wives, juggling their breathing through laughter,
As the funny man danced out in front of them,
Lit so no shadow would fall on him.
It was like looking at the night sky – a spread of echoes.
Events that happened years ago, revealing themselves,
Disclosing their final moments, then disappearing.
Watching the adult stars of my childhood,
Dashing across a black screen, existing in laughter only,
Then silenced, was enough to fill a few minutes of my time,
From their lifetime's achievements.

The Drowned Fields

Although being without him now
would be like standing on one leg
still everything seems paper thin.

If my foot slips and breaks the surface,
I'll fall to a land of drowned fields,
where the only language is the language

of the sky and the birds make endless
patterns in the air and the pools of water
are words the rain has left behind.

The birds are like shadows in the corner
of my eye, or silver, as if the sky
is throwing money to the ground.

Next to the path the grass moves beneath
my feet. Hummocks store black water
while his thoughts, impossible to ignore

push their way across the land like large
enthusiastic dogs. The lives I could
have led are silver threads across

the drowning land and birds come
together, then spread apart, as if the sky
opened its hand and let them loose.

Directions

When you leave the motorway, just keep driving,
south and east, past the castle and on up Lindale Hill.

This is where, on certain nights, the roe deer come.
Fog can make them leap the barrier like horses

High Newton and Low Newton nestle like two fists.
Keep them on your right. You'll see the lights

of Newby Bridge, the hotels lit up for Christmas.
There's the bridge, swallowed by the floods last year,

and the river stole the door of that hotel.
Here is Ulverston. You'll know it by the houses

painted blue and pink, but don't be distracted.
Ignore Dalton on your left, the zoo on your right.

You'll see the lions lolling on their shelves
and the red-skinned rhinoceros like statues.

Many years ago, one escaped and came charging
down this road, before I came to live here.

Keep going, past the factories. When you smell
scented candles turn left and head for town.

I'll meet you in front of the library. If you see
a submarine shed big enough to fit a street

of terraced houses, or a wasteland where something
is waiting to be built, you've come too far. Turn around.

It snowed for twenty years

and the people forgot what the sky
looked like without the thought of snow,
without its whispered threat. They forgot
cars, gave them up to the snow's kindness,
liked how the world looked bigger,
every contour exaggerated with snow.

One great city became a thousand towns
and each town became a hundred villages
and the people began once more to know
each other. Pulley systems linked
each house and food zipped along the wirves
as words had in the old days.

In the tenth year, the snow started to melt.
The air was filled with the deathly crack
of ice and all the things they'd made to cope –
the sleds, the dogs with blue eyes, the wires,
the huge warm barns for sheep and cows
started to take up too much space

without the snow to keep it all apart.
The people came together and prayed
for ten more years of snow, so they
could learn to live without the need
for separation, and the sky took pity
and shook its whisper over the land again.

Biographies

Rachael Allen's poetry has appeared or is forthcoming in *Rising, The Salt Book of Younger Poets* and *The Cadaverine*. She has freelanced for newspapers in the UK and the USA and is a co-founder of clinic.

Hanna Andersson is studying for an MA at Konstfack University College in Stockholm, Sweden. Her work is a mixture of printwork, sculpture, drawings and installations.

Kouhei Ashino is an illustrator and zine-maker living in Tokyo, Japan.

Sophia Augusta is an illustrator and co-founder of PLATS collective.

Alexey Berezkin is a collage artist living in Moscow, Russia.

Harriet Bridgwater graduated with a degree in Fine Art from Falmouth in 2009 and is now a freelance designer and screenprinter from Worcestershire now based in Brighton.

James Brookes lives in rural Sussex. He recieved an Eric Gregory Award in 2009 and a Hawthornden Fellowship in 2011. His pamphlet, *The English Sweats,* was published in 2009; his first collection is forthcoming from Salt.

Sam Buchan-Watts graduated from Goldsmiths College in 2010, and is a co-founder of clinic.

Niall Campbell is from the Western Isles of Scotland and graduated from St Andrews University in 2009 with an MLitt in Creative Writing. His first pamphlet is due to be released by Happenstance Press.

John Challis was born in Essex and is studying for an MA in Creative Writing at Newcastle University. He co-directs Trashed Organ and writes regular reviews for *Hand + Star.*

Kayo Chingonyi's poems have appeared in *Tate Etc.*, *Wasafiri* and *City Lighthouse* (Tall Lighthouse) and are forthcoming in *The Salt Book of Younger Poets*.

Tim Cockburn was raised in Nottingham. He has studied Creative Writing at the Norwich School of Art and Design and the University of East Anglia. He lives and works in Norwich.

Sophie Collins grew up in Holland and graduated from Goldsmiths College in 2010. Her work has appeared in *Mercy* and *Rising*. She lives in London.

Michael Dotson grew up attending art school with his design-student mother; he later returned to the same school for his own education in painting. He lives in Washington DC.

Dai George comes from Cardiff but now lives in Harrow. He's currently working on his first collection. His criticism has appeared or is forthcoming in *The Boston Review*, *The Guardian* and *Poetry Wales*.

Mike Goldby attends Ontario College of Art and Design in Toronto. He works primarily in digital imaging and painting.

Matthew Gregory was educated at Norwich School of Art and Design and Goldsmiths College. He has lived in Prague, St Petersburg and New York. He won an Eric Gregory in 2010 and is currently working on his first collection.

Nathan Hamilton runs Egg Box Publishing and co-edits the *Stop Sharpening Your Knives* anthology series. His poetry and criticism have appeared in *Poetry London*, *The Guardian* and *The Rialto*.

Emily Hasler was born in Felixstowe. Her poems appear or are forthcoming in *The Rialto, Poetry Salzburg* and *The Salt Book of Younger Poets*. In 2009 she came second in the Edwin Morgan International Poetry Competition.

Oli Hazzard is originally from Bristol. His poetry has appeared or is forthcoming in *The Forward Book of Poetry 2010*, *The Salt Book of Younger Poets* and *New Poetries V* (Carcanet). He is currently a postgraduate student at the University of Bristol.

Rob Hope-Johnstone lives and works in Peckham, London

Jack Hudson is an illustrator and designer born and raised in Birmingham, now freelancing in Bristol, England.

Kirsten Irving is co-editor of *Fuselit* and Sidekick Books. Her first pamphlet is forthcoming from Happenstance and her first collection from Salt.

Luke Kennard's second book of poetry, *The Harbour Beyond the Movie,* was shortlisted for the Forward Prize in 2007. His new pamphlet, *Planet-Shaped Horse*, is available now from Nine Arches Press. He lectures at the University of Birmingham.

Amy Key's pamphlet *Instead of Stars* is published by Tall Lighthouse. She co-runs The Shuffle poetry night and her last poetry commission inspired a pair of nipple tassels by designer Holloway-Smith Noir.

Caleb Klaces is originally from Birmingham and is currently based at the University of Texas, Austin. His pamphlet is forthcoming from Flarestack Poets. He is co-founder and editor of online poetry project Likestarlings.

Paul Layzell is an illustrator currently based in Brighton. His recent work is centered on 'the city', specifically looking at New York street culture.

Bob London was born inside a snowglobe on top of Jack and Vera Duckworth's mantelpiece at No. 9 Coronation Street, Manchester. He lives and works in London.

Alex MacDonald was born in Essex and now lives and works in London. He is a former speechwriter and edits the website SelectedPoems.

Edward Mackay's poetry was shortlisted for The Picador Poetry Prize in 2011 and shortlisted for an Eric Gregory Award in 2009.

Toby Martinez de las Rivas received an Eric Gregory award in 2005 and the Andrew Waterhouse award from New Writing North in 2008. His Faber and Faber pamphlet was published in 2009. His poems have appeared in publications in England, America, Slovenia, Spain and Italy. He lives in Cordoba.

Aaron McLaughlin is currently in his third year at Glasgow School of Art.

Harriet Moore has been published in *Magma* and Pomegranate and recorded for PoetCasting. She is in her final year at UCL.

Kim Moore works as a peripatetic brass teacher for Cumbria Music Service and is one of two resident poets for the first Leeds Independent Poetry Press Festival. In 2010 she won the Geoffrey Dearmer Prize.

Olja Oblvco from Moscow, Russia is now a fourth year student of architecture.

Andrew Parkes is studying for an MA in Modern Literary Theory at Goldsmiths College and is a co-founder of clinic.

Aimee Parrot graduated with a BA in Fine Art from University College Falmouth in 2009. She lives in Brighton.

Abigail Parry's poems have appeared in *Ambit* and *The Rialto* and she is at work on a first collection. She won an Eric Gregory in 2010.

Tom Rees completed the BA in Art Practice at Goldsmiths in June 2010. He lives in Peckham.

Declan Ryan was born in Mayo, Eire and lives in North London. He programmes the reading series Days of Roses, and recently co-edited its first anthology.

Sean Roy Parker is a third year Illustration undergraduate at London College of Communication and is a co-founder of clinic.

Jon Stone was born in Derby and currently lives in Whitechapel, where he co-edits both Sidekick Books and arts magazine *Fuselit*. His debut pamphlet, *Scarecrows*, was released by Happenstance in 2009.

Ross Sutherland was born in Edinburgh. His second poetry collection, *Twelve Nudes*, was published by Penned In The Margins in 2010. He is a member of the poetry collective Aisle16, with whom he runs Homework, an evening of literary miscellany in East London.

Jack Teagle graduated from the University of Plymouth in 2009. Primarily drawing and painting comics, his work has featured in 3 solo shows and his first published comic, 'Jeff Job Hunter', was released by Nobrow Press.

Olly Todd's poems have appeared or are forthcoming in *Vice, Plus One* and *Mercy*. He lives in Elephant & Castle and swears by the typewriter.

Patrick Tsai graduated from NYU's Tisch School of the Arts in 2003. His work has been featured in *Foam, Vice* and *Autofocus; The Self-Portrait in Contemporary Photography*. He lives and works in Tokyo.

Jack Underwood graduated from Norwich School of Art and Design and is currently studying towards a PhD in Creative Writing at Goldsmiths College, where he also teaches. He is a librettist, musician and co-edits the anthology series *Stop Sharpening Your Knives*. He won an Eric Gregory Award in 2007.

White White Brown Twig started in a field in 2009, and is the collaborative work of photographer Emma Parry, and graphic artist Ventral Is Golden, currently based in Leeds.

$$\frac{275}{500}$$